My Guide to the
CONSTITUTION

THE EXECUTIVE BRANCH

Bonnie Hinman

Mitchell Lane

PUBLISHERS

P.O. Box 196
Hockessin, Delaware 19707

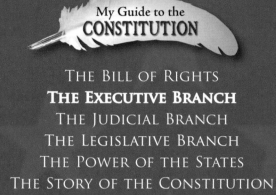

My Guide to the
CONSTITUTION

The Bill of Rights
The Executive Branch
The Judicial Branch
The Legislative Branch
The Power of the States
The Story of the Constitution

Copyright © 2012 by Mitchell Lane Publishers

Printing   2   3   4   5   6   7   8   9

PUBLISHER'S NOTE: The Constitution of the United States appears in the appendix to My Guide to the Constitution: *The Story of the Constitution*. The amendments to the Constitution, including the Bill of Rights, appear in the appendix to My Guide to the Constitution: *The Bill of Rights*.

The facts on which this book is based have been thoroughly researched. Documentation of such research can be found on page 44. While every possible effort has been made to ensure accuracy, the publisher will not assume liability for damages caused by inaccuracies in the data, and makes no warranty on the accuracy of the information contained herein.

**Library of Congress
Cataloging-in-Publication Data**
Hinman, Bonnie.
  The executive branch / by Bonnie Hinman.
     p. cm.—(My guide to the Constitution)
  Includes bibliographical references and index.
  ISBN 978-1-58415-943-8 (library bound)
  1. Presidents—United States—Juvenile literature. 2. Executive power—United States—Juvenile literature. I. Title.
  JK517.H57 2011
  352.230973—dc22

2011002749

Paperback ISBN: 9781612281858

eBook ISBN: 9781612280875

1193

PLB

CONTENTS

Words in **bold** type can be found in the glossary.

Chapter 1

We Elect Our Leader

"The most powerful person in the world"—how often has a reporter said this of the president of the United States? The description is likely true, but the U.S. president still has many limits on his or her power. The founders of the United States of America made sure of this when they wrote the country's constitution. During more than 200 years since 1787 when these founders first met, several presidents have run into trouble over how much power they have.

The members of the "Grand Convention" that met in Philadelphia in May 1787 weren't even supposed to write a new constitution. They were supposed to revise the Articles of Confederation that had been guiding the new American nation since 1781. While the Articles were a constitution, they were not working out for the new nation.

Under the Articles of Confederation, the thirteen colonies that had declared their independence in 1776 were loosely organized. The colonies had suffered under the harsh laws of England's King George III. The delegates at the new convention

King George III

Drafting the Articles of Confederation

York Town, Pennsylvania 1777 13c USA

A commemorative stamp from 1977 illustrates the drafting of the Articles of Confederation.

wanted nothing to do with any government that gave power to one leader. According to the Articles, power was totally in the hands of the states.

There was a president, but he was under the direct supervision of the Congress and could do nothing without its approval. The central government was weak and had trouble doing anything on behalf of the United States as a whole. The Congress could ask the states to send money to pay for an army, for example, but it was powerless if the states said no. Many of the states had their own navies and negotiated their own trade policies with foreign governments.

The Articles limped along as a guide for the new nation until the Revolutionary War was over in 1783. In the years that followed, it became apparent that the United States could not achieve and keep peace and prosperity under the Articles of Confederation. Something had to be done to strengthen the Union.

When the convention met in Philadelphia to revise the Articles, the delegates soon realized that the Articles couldn't be revised enough to work. They would have to write an entirely new constitution.

The final draft of the new constitution was finished in September 1787 but was not **ratified** by the required nine of thirteen states until June 1788. It went into effect in 1789 and has governed the country ever since. The Bill of Rights was added in 1789 and ratified in 1791. Seventeen additional amendments have since been approved. One of the biggest changes from the Articles of Confederation to the new constitution was the establishment of three separate branches of government. The legislative, judicial, and executive branches would share power, and a system of checks and balances would keep any single branch from having more power than the others.

President George Washington closely oversaw the design and construction of the White House in Washington, D.C.

George Washington's first **inauguration** took place in New York City on April 30, 1789. Washington took the oath of office on the balcony of the Federal Hall while a crowd watched from the street below. Then officials moved inside to hear Washington's inaugural speech in the Senate Chamber.

Heading the executive branch is a single person: the president. That person has to be at least 35 years old and be a natural born citizen or have lived in the United States when the Constitution was adopted. He or she must have lived in the United States for at least 14 years. Although women would not be allowed to vote until 1920, the Constitution does not say that only men may be president.

The method used to elect presidents was confusing then and still is, even though the Twelfth Amendment was meant to simplify the process. Registered voters in the United States vote for the presidential candidate of their choice. Winning the popular vote, however, does not ensure that the candidate will be president. Four presidents have been elected without winning the popular vote, including George W. Bush in 2000.

The U.S. Constitution says than an Electoral College will elect the president. Members of the Electoral College are appointed or elected to represent their state. Each state has the same number of electoral votes as it has senators and representatives.

Most states direct their electors to vote for the candidate who won the popular vote in their state. However, in some states the electors can vote however they want.

The 2000 election is a good example of how the electoral process can complicate elections and why many citizens think it would be best to **abolish** the Electoral College. The 2000 presidential election was between Texas Governor George W. Bush and Vice President Al Gore. It was a very close election, and in the end the winner depended on which candidate won Florida's electoral votes.

The winner of the 2000 race for the presidency between Al Gore and George W. Bush came down to who won Florida's 25 electoral votes.

Both candidates complained of flawed voting practices in some Florida counties. Recounts and challenges went on for weeks while the nation had no idea who was going to be the next president. During this time someone in the media or government made up a new term, the "hanging chad." A chad is the tiny piece of paper that is pushed out when a voter punches a hole by a candidate's name. A machine can then count the votes by recording which holes have been punched out. A "hanging chad" happens when the voter does not punch hard enough to make the chad fall out.

Hanging chads became a common term in late 2000 after the presidential election in November. The tiny pieces of paper that refused to fall out when punched in a voting machine were blamed for weeks of delay in naming the winner of the election. This type of ballot was used in Votomatic voting machines.

It appeared that the machines had sometimes incorrectly recorded the votes. Some counties had to recount the votes. Eventually the candidates and their lawyers demanded that the votes be recounted by hand. In that process a person held up each ballot and looked to see which chad had been pushed out. Some chads were hanging, and there were disputes over which candidate the voter had chosen. Should the ballots with the hanging chads be thrown out?

Weeks went by as the votes were counted and recounted and hand-counted and challenged. Meanwhile lawyers for Bush and Gore went from circuit courts to state courts to the U.S. Supreme Court to either stop the counts or continue them. In the end the U.S. Supreme Court decided in favor of stopping the counts. George W. Bush would be the next U.S. president. He had won the Electoral College vote, even though he had not won the popular vote nationwide.

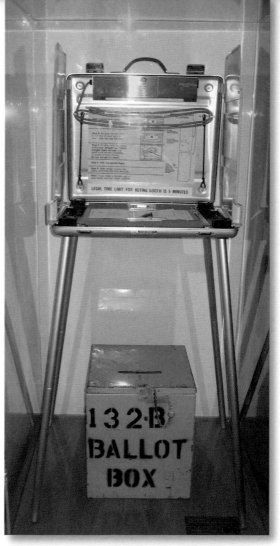

Voting stand, ballot, and ballot box from Palm Beach County, 2000

Originally, the candidate who won the most votes became president, and the one with the next highest number of votes became vice president. This changed in 1804 with the addition of the Twelfth

John Tyler was the first vice president to become president after the death of his predecessor. President William Henry Harrison died on April 4, 1841. Contrary to the common story, Harrison did not catch a cold on his inauguration day. He became ill three weeks later and died of pneumonia a week or so after that.

Amendment. It states that electors must vote separately for president and vice president. Now each presidential candidate chooses a running mate, the person who will be vice president should that candidate win the presidency. Even though the Electoral College officially votes separately for the president and vice president, the running mates are still a team. One cannot be elected without the other.

The president and his vice president serve four-year terms and are limited to two terms of office. The vice president becomes president if the president dies, resigns, or is in some way unable or unwilling to take care of his duties. The original part of the Constitution about the

President Zachary Taylor had never voted in an election before he voted for himself in 1848.

line of succession was made clearer by the Twenty-fifth amendment, which was ratified in 1967. The U.S. Congress establishes the line of succession after the vice president. At present the majority leader of the House of

Representatives, also known as the Speaker of the House, is third in line to become president.

The newly elected president officially takes office on January 20 following the November election. Called Inauguration Day, this is when the new president and vice president take the oath of office on the steps of the U.S. Capitol. The Constitution says that the president shall take the following oath or affirmation. "I do solemnly swear (or affirm) that I will faithfully execute the Office of president of the United States, and will to the best of my ability, preserve, protect and defend the Constitution of the United States."

After the official ceremonies the rest of the day and night are devoted to celebration. There is a grand inaugural parade with bands, floats, and other groups. That night there are many inaugural balls. George Washington started the tradition of holding a ball to celebrate the inauguration.

Now the number of different inaugural balls held that night is in the double digits. The president and his wife usually attend each ball. President Barack Obama's daughters and friends were treated to their own inaugural event in the White House in 2009. The party ended with a surprise visit from the Jonas Brothers.

The office of vice president has often been ridiculed because it has no real duties assigned to it. John Adams was so bored with the office, he complained: "My country has in its wisdom contrived for me the most insignificant office that ever the invention of man contrived or his imagination conceived."[1] On the other hand, Vice President Al Gore (1992–2000) used the office to promote environmental policy and the use of technology. Vice President Dick Cheney (2000–2008) pushed for an expansion of presidential powers. Fourteen vice presidents subsequently became president of the United States.

Chapter 2

Commander in Chief

One of the powers of the executive branch is that of being the commander in chief of the U.S. military. The president is the **civilian** leader of the armed forces. Generals (from the army, air force, and marines) and admirals (from the navy) are in charge of the day-to-day operations of the military, but they must answer to the president.

Even in many modern countries, military leaders may decide that the elected president is not doing his duty and take over the country by force. This cannot happen in the United States because the Constitution states that the president is the ultimate authority over the military.

Presidents take their duty as chief soldier very seriously. They work with military and other national leaders to keep soldiers supplied and as safe as possible. They try to demonstrate to the American people how citizens should respect the soldiers who protect their country at home and in wars far from home.

At the end of the Revolutionary War, General George Washington handed his resignation as the commander in chief of the army to Congress. His action showed support for a democracy rather than a military dictatorship.

President Barack Obama visited the troops at Bagram Airfield in Afghanistan on March 28, 2010.

One way presidents show respect for the armed forces is by visiting them in war zones, such as in Iraq and Afghanistan. These trips encourage the troops and show them how much the president and the people at home appreciate them.

In section 2 of Article II, the Constitution gives the president some other important powers. He is allowed to negotiate treaties and agreements with other countries on behalf of the United States. Treaties can end wars or promise certain trade advantages. These treaties are subject to the approval of the Senate.

After World War I, President Woodrow Wilson made huge efforts to get the Senate to approve a **treaty** that would create the League of Nations. League member countries would agree to defend each other against invasions by other countries in an effort to prevent another world war. In spite of Wilson's efforts, the Senate did not approve the treaty. U.S. leaders after World War I feared that the country would be forced to fight other countries again whether or not it was in the best interest of the United States. The Senate favored **isolationism,** and this belief lingered until the 1940s.

The president can appoint ambassadors and other public officers. For example, he or she appoints the leaders, called secretaries, of important executive branch departments. The group of these fifteen leaders, plus the vice president, is called the cabinet. They advise the president regarding their departments. These departments are Agriculture, Commerce, Defense, Education, Energy, Health and Human Services, Homeland Security, Housing and Urban Development, Interior, Labor, State, Transportation, Treasury, and Veterans Affairs. As head of the Justice Department, the Attorney General is also part of the cabinet. He or she advises the president on legal issues. Once a cabinet leader is appointed, he or she must be approved by the Senate. (Other executive agencies, including the Central Intelligence Agency and the Environmental Protection Agency, are under the authority of the president, but their department heads are not part of the cabinet.)

The president can also make appointments to the Supreme Court. Again, these appointments have to be approved by two-thirds of the Senate members. Hearings are held in the Senate, and the members can speak for or against the prospective public official. Some Supreme Court nominees are not approved. For example, Robert Bork, nominated by President Ronald Reagan in 1987, was rejected. Sometimes the president withdraws the nomination when too much opposition arises, or the candidate withdraws on his or her own. Harriet Miers, nominated by president George W. Bush, withdrew in 2005 after questions arose about her inexperience.

The president is also allowed to grant **pardons** or **reprieves** to persons accused or **convicted** of crimes against the United States. One of the more controversial pardons was the one President Gerald Ford gave former President Richard Nixon. Nixon resigned from office in August 1974 after a long hearing over what was called the Watergate scandal. The Watergate Office Complex in Washington, D.C., was the scene of a burglary in June 1972 at the Democratic National Committee

The Watergate Hotel and Office Complex became forever famous as the site of a burglary in 1972. This burglary and the aftermath led to the downfall of President Richard Nixon in 1974.

headquarters. Accusers thought the burglary was done to help Nixon become president in the 1972 election.

Nixon was accused of helping to cover up the burglary. He resigned when it looked as if he would be impeached (formally charged for high crimes and **misdemeanors**).

If Nixon had been impeached and convicted, Ford would not have been able to use his presidential power to pardon him. The Constitution forbids the president from giving pardons in cases of impeachment and conviction. This prevents any president from pardoning himself should he be impeached and convicted. More directions about removing the president from office were given in section 4 of Article II of the Constitution.

Another power granted to the president in Article II, section 2 is the right to make recess appointments—which means he or she can fill vacancies while the Senate is not in session. Communication was poor in the 1780s, and travel was difficult and time-consuming, so it made sense to allow the president to make these appointments during these recesses. These appointees could serve only until the end of the next Senate session.

Modern presidents have sometimes used this power to name officials they suspect may not be approved by the Senate. While the public often complains about this power, it is expressly given in the Constitution, and only an amendment can change it.

The powers given to the president in section 2 seem few when viewed from a modern perspective. Citizens know that presidents have many more powers than those mentioned in section 2. The Constitution authors made this list short on purpose. Many of the framers worried about giving too much power to one person. This short list of given powers helped those delegates support the new Constitution. It was up to the presidents to decide how to employ their powers and which powers could safely be added to their roles.

The first president, George Washington, did a great deal to model the kind of president the United States should have. He was a strong leader and projected that he, rather than the states or Congress, was in charge. He believed in the power of symbols and approved the design of the White House to be grand but not like a palace. He refused to be addressed as any other than Mr. President, rejecting Your Highness or other royal titles. He started the tradition of the president sitting for a portrait. He also took trips throughout the states to show everyone that the new United States had a strong leader.

As the nation and the government expanded, so did the powers and the duties of the president.

The Executive Office employs over 1,800 people; the executive branch, which includes the armed forces, employs over 4 million people.

Chapter 3

Head of State

The U.S. president is considered the head of state as well as the head of government. Many countries have a different system that divides duties between two people. Great Britain has a queen as head of state and a prime minister as head of government. Germany has a president and a chancellor. Russia has a president and a premier.

In general the head of state might handle many of the ceremonial duties while the head of government takes charge of the actual running of the country. The United States vests both of these duties in the president—although the vice president may stand in as head of state should the president be tied up with other duties.

U.S. presidents are sometimes called the encouragers of state because they are often called upon to talk to citizens about disasters, wars, economic troubles, and many other worrisome topics. The president encourages and reassures the people that the nation is strong and will overcome its problems.

G-20 (Group of Twenty) world leaders met on April 2, 2009, for the London Summit. The focus of the summit was the global financial crisis and how to reverse it. Leaders attending included U.S. President Barack Obama, British Prime Minister Gordon Brown, and Queen Elizabeth of England.

Fires burned at the World Trade Center shortly before the Twin Towers collapsed on September 11, 2001.

On September 11, 2001, terrorists attacked and destroyed the Twin Towers in New York City; damaged the Pentagon in Washington, D.C.; and crashed a jetliner in the Pennsylvania countryside. Thousands of people died that day in a disaster such as the country had never seen before. President George W. Bush spoke often to the people in the days that followed the attacks. He reassured citizens that the country would survive and become stronger. He promised that the terrorist organizations that had mounted the attacks would be caught and punished.

To encourage U.S. citizens after the disaster, President Bush stood on a pile of rubble at the site of the Twin Towers. He used a bullhorn to talk to the rescuers and workers. Some of the workers shouted that they couldn't hear him. Bush replied, "I can hear you! I can hear you! The rest of the world hears you! And the people—and the people who knocked these buildings down will hear all of us soon!"[1]

The Constitution instructs the president to give information to the Congress from time to time. Although not specified in the Constitution, this duty is traditionally fulfilled when the president gives a State of the Union address to a joint session of Congress. This takes place in January in all years when there is not a new president. The president talks about his accomplishments over the past year and details plans for the new year. Occasionally the president announces new programs or ideas that he hopes to implement.

The Constitution instructs the president to recommend measures that he or she thinks are necessary for the good of the nation. The president can say what he hopes to accomplish, but it is the Congress who approves the measures or makes the laws.

The two houses of Congress may or may not vote to pass laws or proposals from the president. If a bill is passed in the House of Representatives and the Senate, it must be signed by the president before it becomes law. In a check to legislative power, the president can veto, or refuse to sign, a bill. The bill then goes back to the body, House or Senate, that sent it to the president. Those members can vote to override the veto and make the bill a law even though the president rejected it. A two-thirds majority from both the House and the Senate is required to override the veto.

The president may also call for a special session of Congress if he thinks it is necessary to pass a certain law by a certain time. The Constitution says that the reasons for this must be "on extraordinary occasions." Harry S. Truman called a special session of Congress in 1948 to ask for legislation on housing, civil rights, and extended social security. This was seen as a political move made by Truman to help him win the 1948 presidential election (which he did).

Many world leaders visit the U.S. president to talk with him about various issues, but they may also come for a formal State Visit. There are special arrival ceremonies and other events during a State Visit. The highlight is usually the State Dinner, which is a lavish party designed to please the visiting head of state. For the dozens of dignitaries invited, attending a State Dinner is a great honor.

William Howard Taft was the first president to throw the ceremonial first pitch in baseball, something every president has done ever since (with the exception of Jimmy Carter).

The president also meets with sports heroes and other stars. Traditionally the president invites baseball's World Series winners to the White House, and he telephones winners of the Olympics and other special groups. He or she also meets with veterans, Eagle Scouts, authors, volleyball teams, and other citizens groups.

A less-used power given in section 3 is the president's right to adjourn Congress if the two houses can't agree on a date. Congress did not meet year-round in the early years, so there may have been disagreements about adjournment when a congressman wanted to have a vote on an issue before the session ended.

The president traditionally pardons a Thanksgiving turkey every year. Two turkeys are chosen for the event in case one of them gets sick. Both lucky birds are sent to live out their lives as celebrities in such places as Mount Vernon or Disneyland.

Finally in section 3, the president is directed to "take care that the laws be faithfully executed." How the president is to do this is not spelled out in the Constitution. This may have been another example of the framers leaving out the details on purpose so as not to rile those opposed to a strong central government, and to leave the government flexible enough to adapt to the future.

To be sure that laws are followed, the president may intervene with law enforcement, though this has rarely happened. In 1957, President Dwight D. Eisenhower used this power during the forced integration of schools in Little Rock, Arkansas. The U.S. Supreme Court had ruled that having separate schools for black and white children was unconstitutional. When Little Rock was slow to integrate the schools, Eisenhower sent in federal troops to make sure that the law was followed. The president can also activate individual state militias if disasters or other disturbances threaten the peace and property of U.S. citizens. He does not have to have Congressional approval to do this. President George W. Bush was criticized for not sending troops to New Orleans quickly enough after Hurricane Katrina devastated the Gulf Coast in 2005.

Hungarian immigrant author Stefan Lorant described the American presidency as a "glorious burden."[2] Observers have often commented that the presidency seems to age the person toiling under this "glorious burden," and it is likely they are right. The president's powers and duties have increased greatly in the last 100 years. The job would wear anyone out.

In 1844, Julia Tyler, second wife of president John Tyler, instructed the Marine band to play "Hail to the Chief" when the president made a ceremonial entry. This custom has persisted to the present.

Chapter 4

Impeachment

Impeachment is the most serious check on the power of the president and other officers of the government; it is rarely used. Impeachment is not the removal of a president from office but the process that must be followed for him or her to be removed.

Section 4 of Article II states: "The president, vice president and all civil officers of the United States, shall be removed from office on impeachment for and conviction of treason, bribery, or other high crimes and misdemeanors." This wording leaves a lot to interpretation. Although *treason* and *bribery* are legally accepted terms, opinions vary widely about what constitutes high crimes and misdemeanors. Are "high crimes" only those offenses that can be tried in court? Or are there other serious actions a president might take that might not be listed as "criminal actions"? Constitutional experts, lawyers, and politicians have long argued over these questions.

Supreme Court Chief Justice Salmon P. Chase presided over the impeachment trial of President Andrew Johnson. Senate members served as the jury for the trial, which started on March 13, 1868.

Vice President Andrew Johnson became president in 1865. He stirred up trouble because he wanted to forgive the Confederate leaders after the Civil War. Many U.S. citizens and leaders did not agree with that plan.

Impeachment proceedings begin in the House of Representatives. Any member of the House may start the impeachment process by introducing a **resolution** to that effect. The House **Judiciary** Committee conducts hearings and investigations into the supposed wrongdoing or abuse of power. The committee decides whether or not to submit the resolution to the entire House of Representatives. If the committee does send the resolution and the whole House votes, a simple majority of votes is needed to approve the resolution and impeach the president.

The trial for the president is held in the Senate. Selected members of the House act as prosecutors, and Senate members serve as judge and jury. After all testimonies and evidence have been heard, Senate members vote yes or no to remove the president from office. Two-thirds of the Senate members present must vote in favor of conviction for the president to be removed.

The impeachment process has been carried through to its final stages only two times in U.S. history. The first president to be impeached was Andrew Johnson in 1868. President Bill Clinton was impeached in December 1998. Impeachment articles had been drawn up against President Richard Nixon in 1974, but he resigned before they could be executed.

Andrew Johnson became president when Abraham Lincoln was **assassinated** in 1865. Johnson had been selected to run as Lincoln's vice president even though Johnson was a Democrat and Lincoln was a Republican. President Johnson argued with Congress regularly about how the **Reconstruction** of the defeated South should proceed. He vetoed or rejected almost all the ideas Congress put forward. Supreme Court Justice David Davis said that President Johnson was "obstinate, self-willed, combative" and unfit to be president.[1]

Few members of Congress would have minded if Johnson had disappeared, but being obstinate and combative was not grounds for impeachment. At last President Johnson pushed the Congress too hard in his attempt to wield power. He removed Secretary of War Edwin Stanton and planned to appoint someone who was friendlier to the president's plans to stop Reconstruction. This proved to be Johnson's undoing, because according to the rules at that time, cabinet members could not be fired without the approval of Congress.

At last the Congress had legitimate reasons to impeach the increasingly irritating Johnson. The Senate trial of Andrew Johnson began in 1868.

The actual removal of Johnson would not have been the perfect solution, because there was no vice president to take his place. According to the rules at that time, the presidency would go to the Senate president **pro tem.** Ben Wade, who held that office, had radical opinions about Reconstruction. Republicans weren't sure that a Ben Wade presidency would be any better than an Andrew Johnson one.

Johnson escaped conviction by one vote, and he served out the remainder of his term. Most of the Republicans who went against their party and voted to acquit him shared his views on Reconstruction policies.

President Bill Clinton's impeachment in 1998 was almost entirely argued on the basis of the definitions of what were "high crimes and misdemeanors." Clinton supporters said that while the president may have acted unwisely, his actions did not rise to the level of high crimes and misdemeanors.

President Clinton's problems had started before he became president. There had been accusations that he mishandled some legal matters and that, even though he was married, he secretly met women for romantic purposes. Nothing was ever proven, and Clinton's

President Clinton signed the Education Flexibility Partnership Act of 1999 at a ceremony on April 29, 1999. Most presidents follow an old tradition of signing bills into law with a number of different pens. The pens are then presented to the bill's supporters as souvenirs.

presidency had success in dealing with issues of free trade, balancing the national budget, and reforming the welfare system.

His earlier problems resurfaced, however, when it was discovered that the president had engaged in a romantic relationship with a White House **intern** named Monica Lewinsky. At first Clinton denied the claims about his relationship with her. Later he admitted that while he may have acted unwisely, he did not do anything criminal. That is when the debate began over what kinds of actions are high crimes and misdemeanors.

Eventually Clinton was accused of obstruction of justice and **perjury** because he had lied under oath to a grand jury. The idea took hold that it wasn't so much what he did that was worthy of being impeached, but rather the fact that he had lied about his actions.

President Clinton's case went to the Senate for trial in January 1999. He had a better result than Johnson when the votes came in. Although almost half of the senators voted to convict President Clinton on the two charges, the Constitution demands a two-third's majority to convict. He was acquitted and served out the remainder of his term.

Presidential impeachment is a distracting and serious process for the country to endure. It is, however, an essential part of the Constitution that limits presidential power. No president wants to undergo such a process. The possibility of impeachment helps a president think carefully about his actions while in office.

An unexplained eighteen-minute gap in a recording made in President Nixon's office on June 20, 1972, three days after the Watergate burglary, was a condemning piece of evidence against the president. It appeared that Nixon or his chief of staff intentionally erased the tape because it held evidence that Nixon knew about the break-in before it happened.

Chapter 5
How Presidents Live

It isn't easy being a president, as several holders of that office have said. Thomas Jefferson said that presidency was "a place of splendid misery."[1] John Quincy Adams said that he could "scarcely conceive a more harassing, wearying, teasing condition of existence."[2] Outspoken president Harry Truman said, "Being a president is like riding a tiger. A man has to keep on riding or be swallowed."[3] Yet the presidency is an eagerly sought after position.

How presidents spend their days while at work or on vacation has been as different as the men themselves. But they would likely all agree to one fact: They attend meeting after meeting after meeting.

President Barack Obama's daily schedule is similar to those of other recent presidents. On an ordinary day, President Obama will eat breakfast with his family, scan some newspapers, and see his daughters, Malia and Sasha, off to school. Then he goes to the

President Obama reads or skims several
newspapers each morning to find out
what's happening in the world.

third-floor gym to work out before heading downstairs to the Oval Office and officially beginning his workday.

There are a couple of meetings—or briefings, as the White House calls them. These everyday events are usually scheduled in the mornings. First comes the President's Daily Briefing, held with Vice President Joe Biden, the national security adviser, and the director of national intelligence. This and other briefings bring the president up to date on any issues that have come up since the previous day.

When there is time, Obama will meet with his speechwriters or other advisers. He often has a short public event before lunchtime. After lunch, which he often eats in the Oval Office, there will be more meetings with cabinet or congressional members. Occasionally the president will make a statement to the press. He might meet individually with Secretary of State Hillary Clinton, for example. At the end of the day the president will have a very short wrap-up meeting with his chief of staff.

President Obama often meets with Secretary of State Hillary Clinton in the Oval Office. The Secretary of State represents the United States in managing affairs with other countries.

By 6:00 or 6:30, Obama goes back to the family quarters upstairs, where he has dinner with his daughters and wife, Michelle. After dinner the president and his daughters may play with the family dog, Bo, and then it's bath and bedtime for the girls. By 8:30 the president is back at work in his upstairs office reading a nightly briefing book that has been prepared by staff members and delivered after dinner. He reads and e-mails questions and comments to his advisers well into the night.

The security of the president is the responsibility of the Secret Service, one of the most visible parts of the presidential lifestyle. The familiar dark-suited men in sunglasses who never smile are almost always within a few feet of the president in public.

It hasn't always been standard procedure to guard the presidents. Many of the early presidents thought that bodyguards put too much distance between the president and the people who elected him.

The first reported **breach** of presidential security wasn't really a breach because there was no White House security at the time. John Adams, the second president, ran into a deranged man in the newly opened White House. The man threatened to kill Adams. Adams invited the man into his office and calmed him down. The president never called for help.

Four presidents have been assassinated in U.S. history, and there have been assassination attempts on eight others. No special efforts were made to protect presidents until after three assassinations. Even then the protection was minimal.

The first presidential detail to protect the president was made up of two agents who guarded president Theodore Roosevelt. Roosevelt had become president after William McKinley was assassinated in 1901. Roosevelt wrote in a letter to Senator Henry Cabot Lodge that he considered the Secret Service a "very small but very necessary thorn in the flesh."[4]

In 1950, President Harry Truman was living in Blair House while repairs were made to the White House. On November 1, two gunmen protesting about Puerto Rican independence were shot in a gunfight

The Secret Service was formed in 1865 to hunt down money counterfeiters. As such it was part of the Treasury Department. The Secret Service was given the permanent job of protecting presidents in 1902. In 2003, supervision of the Secret Service was transferred to the Department of Homeland Security.

with Secret Service officers while the president took a nap upstairs. One of the protesters and a Secret Service agent later died of injuries from that gunfight.

The assassination of President John F. Kennedy changed how presidents were protected. Apparently the route taken by Kennedy's motorcade required that the vehicles slow down to 11 miles an hour. This slow speed helped the assassin, Lee Harvey Oswald, fire the fatal shots accurately. Today the Secret Service considers routes very carefully ahead of time. The president rides in a bulletproof car, with the windows closed.

Even though Secret Service protection of the president has been ramped up in recent years, assassination attempts are still made. President Ronald Reagan almost died of a chest wound he received during an attempt just after he took office. Secret Service agent Timothy McCarthy was hit in the abdomen while trying to protect him.

Life for presidents and their families is not always one long day after another of being cooped up in the White House and being told what they can't do. Presidents almost always have places they can go to relax. They occasionally continue to do business while there.

George Washington had his estate of Mount Vernon in Virginia, which he visited at least fifteen times during his two terms in office. He stayed from a few days up to several months at Mount Vernon. From there, he tended to presidential business through letters, and he spent time taking care of his farm.

Abraham Lincoln's retreat was less well known. He spent many summer months commuting thirty minutes north of the White House to stay at the Soldiers' Home. The Soldiers' Home was a complex of cottages and buildings where injured soldiers lived. A steady stream of generals, cabinet members, congressmen, and other friends visited him at his retreat.

Franklin Roosevelt vacationed and worked at the family estate at Hyde Park, New York. The train trip from Washington, D.C., took seven

The Soldiers' Home was Lincoln's favorite retreat.

to ten hours. By the time of his presidency, security was much tighter for presidents. The arrangements for him to travel to his retreat involved hundreds of people. The most famous visitors to Hyde Park were probably Winston Churchill, plus King George VI with his wife, Elizabeth, of England. Churchill and Roosevelt met several times to discuss war plans and the atomic bomb.

Roosevelt also authorized the building of a retreat 60 miles north of Washington, D.C., in Maryland's Catoctin Mountains. He named it Shangri-La, but President Dwight Eisenhower renamed it Camp David in honor of his grandson. The retreat is a half-hour helicopter hop from the White House. This rustic collection of cottages and lodges has been the scene of many important presidential decisions for over sixty years.

All presidents since Roosevelt have visited Camp David. Lyndon Johnson made decisions there about the **escalation** of the Vietnam War. As the Watergate scandal was breaking, Nixon asked his two closest advisers to resign while at Camp David.

Jimmy Carter brokered a Middle East deal between Israel and Egypt at Camp David during twelve days of intense talks there in September 1978. In 1990 at Camp David, George H. W. Bush and his senior advisers decided to enter the Gulf War. Bill Clinton presided over a somewhat less successful Middle East summit at Camp David between Palestinian leader Yasser Arafat and Israeli Prime Minister Ehud Barak.

George W. Bush went to Camp David the weekend after the September 11, 2001, terrorist attacks against the United States. He met with his aides to decide how to proceed in the effort to oust the Taliban with its terrorists in Afghanistan. He was also known for taking breaks in Kennebunkport, Maine, and at his homestead in Crawford, Texas, where he spent more than 400 days of his presidency.[5]

Lists of the worst presidents and the best presidents frequently pop up in the media. Sometimes a president can be on both lists, depending on when the survey is made. Presidents are often evaluated differently after they have been out of office for a few years. Most lists have Lincoln or Washington at the top of the best executives. Lincoln was a dedicated

CAMP DAVID

Twelve-year-old
David Eisenhower
became the
namesake for Camp
David. His
grandfather,
President Dwight
Eisenhower, renamed
the presidential
retreat after him.

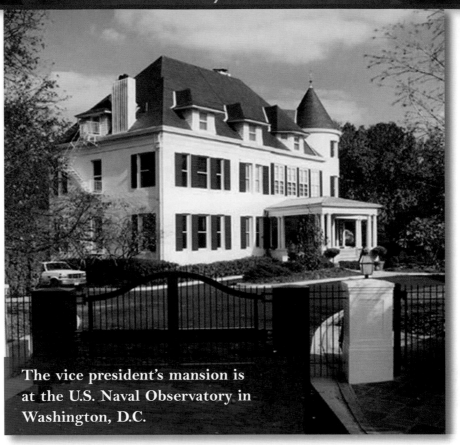

The vice president's mansion is at the U.S. Naval Observatory in Washington, D.C.

and wise leader of the country during the Civil War, one of the darkest times the United States has ever endured.

There's no disputing Lincoln's unique suitability for the job at that time. But if we look at the Constitution and the government it produced, no man was better for the country than George Washington. The authors of the Constitution must have had Washington in mind when they penned Article II about the executive branch.

The founders feared creating a king with too much authority. Washington had no desire to obtain power. The fact that he willingly retired from office after two terms is proof of that. There were no term limits then, so he could have stayed president for the rest of his life, as long as he remained popular.

Washington knew that how a leader of a brand-new country presented himself was important in order to gain respect. He carefully built the image of the presidency to show that the United States was worthy of respect.

Henry Lee III, father of Confederate general Robert E. Lee, gave a eulogy at George Washington's funeral in 1799. His famous words seem as true today as they did then. Lee said that Washington was "first in war, first in peace, and first in the hearts of his countrymen."

While Washington was a great president for his time, there have been many presidents since who have done monumental things for the country. We can be certain that in the future there will be many more men and women who desire to serve their country by being the best presidents possible for their times.

Dolley Madison

There have been many great first ladies, or hostesses of the White House. Most of the first ladies have been the wife of a president (some of the presidents were not married). First ladies oversee ceremonies and social events at the White House, and many of them have also volunteered for specific causes. Dolley Madison (1809–1817) worked to help orphans and women, Rosalynn Carter (1977–1981) was active for people with mental disabilities, and Michelle Obama (2009–) has promoted volunteerism and child nutrition.

President	Vice President
1. George Washington (1789–1797)	John Adams (1789–1797)
2. John Adams (1797–1801)	Thomas Jefferson (1797–1801)
3. Thomas Jefferson (1801–1809)	Aaron Burr (1801–1805)
	George Clinton (1805–1809)
4. James Madison (1809–1817)	George Clinton (1809–1812)
	none (1812–1813)
	Elbridge Gerry (1813–1814)
	none (1814–1817)
5. James Monroe (1817–1825)	Daniel D. Tompkins (1817–1825)
6. John Quincy Adams (1825–1829)	John C. Calhoun (1825–1829)
7. Andrew Jackson (1829–1837)	John C. Calhoun (1829–1832)
	none (1832–1833)
	Martin Van Buren (1833–1837)
8. Martin Van Buren (1837–1841)	Richard M. Johnson (1837–1841)
9. William Henry Harrison (1841)	John Tyler (1841)
10. John Tyler (1841–1845)	none (1841–1845)
11. James K. Polk (1845–1849)	George M. Dallas (1845–1849)
12. Zachary Taylor (1849–1850)	Millard Fillmore (1849–1850)
13. Millard Fillmore (1850–1853)	none (1850–1853)
14. Franklin Pierce (1853–1857)	William King (1853)
	none (1853–1857)
15. James Buchanan (1857–1861)	John C. Breckinridge (1857–1861)
16. Abraham Lincoln (1861–1865)	Hannibal Hamlin (1861–1865)
	Andrew Johnson (1865)
17. Andrew Johnson (1865–1869)	none (1865–1869)
18. Ulysses S. Grant (1869–1877)	Schuyler Colfax (1869–1873)
	Henry Wilson (1873–1875)
	none (1875–1877)
19. Rutherford B. Hayes (1877–1881)	William Wheeler (1877–1881)
20. James A. Garfield (1881)	Chester Arthur (1881)
21. Chester Arthur (1881–1885)	none (1881–1885)
22. Grover Cleveland (1885–1889)	Thomas Hendricks (1885)
	none (1885–1889)
23. Benjamin Harrison (1889–1893)	Levi P. Morton (1889–1893)
24. Grover Cleveland (1893–1897)	Adlai E. Stevenson (1893–1897)
25. William McKinley (1897–1901)	Garret Hobart (1897–1899)
	none (1899–1901)
	Theodore Roosevelt (1901)
26. Theodore Roosevelt (1901–1909)	none (1901–1905)
	Charles Fairbanks (1905–1909)
27. William Howard Taft (1909–1913)	James S. Sherman (1909–1912)
	none (1912–1913)
28. Woodrow Wilson (1913–1921)	Thomas R. Marshall (1913–1921)
29. Warren G. Harding (1921–1923)	Calvin Coolidge (1921–1923)
30. Calvin Coolidge (1923–1929)	none (1923–1925)
	Charles Dawes (1925–1929)

APPENDIX: U.S. PRESIDENTS

President	Vice President
31. Herbert Hoover (1929–1933)	Charles Curtis (1929–1933)
32. Franklin D. Roosevelt (1933–1945)	John Nance Garner (1933–1941)
	Henry A. Wallace (1941–1945)
	Harry S. Truman (1945)
33. Harry S. Truman (1945–1953)	none (1945–1949)
	Alben Barkley (1949–1953)
34. Dwight D. Eisenhower (1953–1961)	Richard Nixon (1953–1961)
35. John F. Kennedy (1961–1963)	Lyndon B. Johnson (1961–1963)
36. Lyndon B. Johnson (1963–1969)	none (1963–1965)
	Hubert Humphrey (1965–1969)
37. Richard Nixon (1969–1974)	Spiro Agnew (1969–1973)
	none (1973)
	Gerald Ford (1973–1974)
38. Gerald Ford (1974–1977)	none (August–December 1974)
	Nelson Rockefeller (1974–1977)
39. Jimmy Carter (1977–1981)	Walter Mondale (1977–1981)
40. Ronald Reagan (1981–1989)	George H. W. Bush (1981–1989)
41. George H. W. Bush (1989–1993)	Dan Quayle (1989–1993)
42. Bill Clinton (1993–2001)	Al Gore (1993–2001)
43. George W. Bush (2001–2009)	Dick Cheney (2001–2009)
44. Barack Obama (2009–)	Joe Biden (2009–)

CHAPTER NOTES

Chapter 1. We Elect Our Leader
1. The White House: Presidents—"John Adams (1797–1801),"
   http://www.whitehouse.gov/about/presidents/johnadams
Chapter 3. Head of State
1. George Bush, "Bullhorn Address to Ground Zero Rescue Workers," *American Rhetoric,* September 14, 2001, http://www.americanrhetoric.com/speeches/gwbush911groundzerobullhorn.htm
2. Lonnie G. Bunch III, Spencer R. Crew, Mark G. Hirsch, and Harry R. Rubenstein, *The American Presidency; A Glorious Burden* (Washington, D.C.: Smithsonian Institution Press, 2000), p. xvii.
Chapter 4. Impeachment
1. Eric Foner, *Reconstruction; America's Unfinished Revolution; 1863–1877* (New York: Harper & Row, Publishers, 1988), p. 335.
Chapter 5. How Presidents Live
1. Lonnie G. Bunch III, Spencer R. Crew, Mark G. Hirsch, and Harry R. Rubenstein, *The American Presidency; A Glorious Burden* (Washington, D.C.: Smithsonian Institution Press, 2000), p. xii.
2. Ibid.
3. Ibid., p. 70.
4. Ronald Kessler, *In the President's Secret Service* (New York: Crown Publishers, 2009), p. 5.
5. Julie Mason, "Bush on Track to Become the Vacation President," *Houston Chronicle,* August 9, 2007, http://www.chron.com/disp/story.mpl/metropolitan/mason/5042364.html

BOOKS

Bausum, Ann. *Our Country's Presidents.* Washington, D.C.: National Geographic Society, 2009.

Cheney, Lynne. *We the People: The Story of Our Constitution.* New York: Simon & Schuster, 2008.

Davis, Kenneth C. *Don't Know Much About the Presidents.* New York: HarperCollins, 2009.

Davis, Todd, and Marc Frey. *The New Big Book of U.S. Presidents.* Philadelphia: Running Press Kids, 2009.

Eccleston, Linda. *When I Grow Up I Want to Be President: A Young Person's Guide to Understanding the Presidency of the United States.* Seattle: CreateSpace, 2009.

Thomas, William Davis. *What Are the Parts of the Government?* Pleasantville, New York: Gareth Stevens Publisher, 2008.

WORKS CONSULTED

Beschloss, Michael. *Presidential Courage; Brave Leaders and How They Changed America, 1789–1989.* New York: Simon & Schuster, 2007.

Bunch, Lonnie G. III, Spencer R. Crew, Mark G. Hirsch, and Harry R. Rubenstein. *The American Presidency; A Glorious Burden.* Washington, D.C.: Smithsonian Institution Press, 2000.

Bush, George. "Bullhorn Address to Ground Zero Rescue Workers," *American Rhetoric,* September 14, 2001. http://www.americanrhetoric.com/speeches/gwbush911groundzerobullhorn.htm

Constitutional Topic: Checks and Balances http://usconstitution.net/consttop_cnb.html

Cronin, Thomas E., and Michael A. Genovese. *The Paradoxes of the American Presidency.* New York: Oxford University Press, 1998.

Foner, Eric. *Reconstruction; America's Unfinished Revolution: 1863–1877.* New York: Harper & Row, 1988.

Kane, Joseph Nathan, Janet Podell, and Steven Anzovin. *Facts About the President from George Washington to George W. Bush.* New York: The H. W. Wilson Company, 2001.

Kessler, Ronald. *In the President's Secret Service.* New York: Crown Publishers, 2009.

Lott, Jeremy. *The Warm Bucket Brigade.* Nashville: Thomas Nelson, 2007.

McPherson, James M., General Editor. *To the Best of My Ability.* London: Dorling Kindersley Publishing, Inc., 2000.

Mason, Julie. "Bush on Track to Become the Vacation President." *Houston Chronicle,* August 9, 2007. http://www.chron.com/disp/story.mpl/metropolitan/mason/5042364.html

O'Brien, Cormac. *Secret Lives of the U.S. Presidents.* Philadelphia: Quirk Books, 2004.

Rybicki, Elizabeth. "Veto Override Procedure in the House and Senate," June 19, 2010.

Saslow, Eli. "A Day in the Life of the President," *Washington Post,* March 2, 2009. http://www.chron.com/disp/story.mpl/nation/6288901.html

Stadelmann, Marcus. *U.S. Presidents for Dummies.* New York: Hungry Minds, Inc., 2002.

Thomas, Helen, and Craig Crawford. *Listen Up, Mr. President.* New York: Scribner, 2009.

The United States Constitution http://www.usconstitution.net/const.html

Walsh, Kenneth. *From Mount Vernon to Crawford.* New York: Hyperion, 2005.

Waterman, Richard W., Robert Wright, and Gilbert St. Clair. *The Image-Is-Everything Presidency.* Boulder, Colorado: Westview Press, 1999.

Watterson, John Sayle. *The Games Presidents Play.* Baltimore: The Johns Hopkins University Press, 2006.

ON THE INTERNET

Congress for Kids: The Executive Branch
    http://www.congressforkids.net/Executivebranch_index.htm
George Washington's Mount Vernon Estate and Gardens
    http://www.mountvernon.org/
If You Were President
    http://www.scholastic.com/kids/president/game.htm
National Archives: Charters of Freedom
    http://www.archives.gov/exhibits/charters/
The White House
    http://www.whitehouse.gov/

abolish (uh-BAH-lish)—To do away with; to make illegal.

assassinate (uh-SAS-ih-nayt)—To murder for political reasons.

breach—A break or tear.

civilian (sih-VIL-yun)—Anyone who is not an active law enforcement officer or member of the armed forces.

convicted (kun-VIK-ted)—Found guilty.

escalation (es-kuh-LAY-shun)—The rapid growth of a plan or operation.

inauguration (in-awg-yur-AY-shun)—The ceremony that marks the beginning of a term in office.

intern (IN-turn)—A person, often a student, who works temporarily in a particular field in order to gain experience in that field.

isolationism (eye-soh-LAY-shuh-nizm)—The policy of a country to stay out of political or economic relationships with other countries.

judiciary (joo-DIH-shee-ayr-ee)—Having to do with the courts, judges, and any other offices that administer justice.

line of succession (suk-SEH-shun)—The order in which executive power is passed down should the president be incapable of carrying out his or her duties.

misdemeanor (MIS-deh-mee-nur)—A crime that is considered a minor offense.

pardon (PAR-dun)—To release a person from further punishment for a crime.

perjury (PER-jur-ee)—A lie told in a court of law.

pro tem (pro TEM)—Short for *pro tempore,* which means "for the time being"; temporary.

ratify (RAT-ih-fy)—To officially approve.

Reconstruction (ree-kun-STRUK-shun)—In American history, the time period right after the Civil War when the states that had seceded were becoming part of the Union again.

reprieve (ruh-PREEV)—A delay in punishment.

resolution (reh-zuh-LOO-shun)—A formal statement that can be voted on by an official body, such as Congress.

treaty (TREE-tee)—A formal agreement between two or more nations.

ABOUT THE AUTHOR

Bonnie Hinman has written more than twenty-five books for young people, including books about the Massachusetts Bay Colony, William Penn, and Benjamin Banneker. She first studied the U.S. Constitution in elementary school and wondered how such a short document could govern the entire United States. She was glued to the television the weekend after President John F. Kennedy was assassinated. She also spent many hours watching the Watergate conspiracy unravel on television in 1974, and the impeachment of Bill Clinton in 1998 and 1999. Hinman lives in Southwest Missouri with her husband, Bill, near her children and five grandchildren.

OCT 2017